Alimony For The Single Daddy

A Short Guide To Understanding Alimony

Nick Thomas

Visit my website at www.singledaddydating.com

ISBN-13: 978-1505405675

ISBN-10: 150540567X

JOIN OUR COMMUNITY!

Single Daddy Dating is a growing community of single fathers who look to help each other, not only with dating success but in all areas of their lives too. This includes parenting, career and finances advice.

Join us today and get '**10 Crucial Checklist To Dating Success For Single Fathers**' completely FREE!

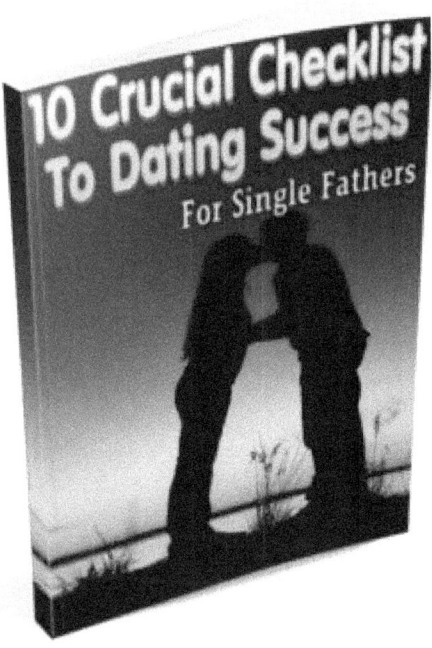

JOIN US AT
WWW.SINGLEDADDYDATING.COM/
NEWSLETTER/

CONTENTS

Chapter 1: Introduction To Alimony

Do you think divorce is fair?

Having met many single fathers over the past few years, I can rightfully vouch that divorce laws in most countries do nothing to make it fair. In fact, it can be so unfair to men that a man may find his post-divorce life so miserable.

This is simply because of the nature of society. Divorce laws, in the past, were created to help protect the rights of women. Many women get into marriages and stay at home to take care of the children. After a divorce, it makes it hard for her to go out to make a living again as she wouldn't have the work experience to go out and make money.

All her time in the past has been focused at home. Traditionally, the wife has been focused at home. For her to go out and find for work post-divorce would make it very difficult. That seem to be the conventional logic for the argument of alimony payments from the man to his ex-wife.

However, things have changed drastically now. Nowadays, women are very often found in the working world too. Traditional stay-at-home mums are getting fewer. Many of the children are sent to day care. In the working world, you would often find that women and men are equal in the workforce.

So, why is there still a notion that women need to be protected?

Alimony, to me, is something that often result in a lot of debate in single father support group meetings. Some men get resentful when thinking about alimony while some treat alimony like something that they should rightfully pay. Some fathers are simply resentful because they have been crippled by the heavy burden of alimony.

When I hear stories from men who are resentful, I understand their situation. Some men have to pay around 50% of their income to the ex-wife each month. The ex-wife would do nothing at home but would get this amount while the man would need to work his butt off.

No wonder so many men are resentful.

For many men, the mere thought of alimony brings scary thoughts. I have seen men whose life gets ripped apart because of alimony. One of them was Ryan, a 53 year old single father from Bemidji, Minnesota. He sent me an email a few years back telling about his misery and how his divorce sent him into depression.

He got a divorce at the age of fifty, twenty years into his marriage with his wife. Things were difficult for many years, but it reached tipping point after their twentieth anniversary. They had three children and the youngest was fifteen at the age of divorce.

His ex-wife, Nadia, was brought up in a wealthy family in New York while Ryan was from a conservative family in Minnesota. Their marriage started off well when they stayed in New York, where Ryan went for his university. A few years after marriage, Ryan decided that that the cost of living in New York was too high, he decided to move back to Minnesota. This was to the dismay of Nadia.

From then on, their marriage took a turn for the worse. By then, the three children were already born and Nadia had no choice but to follow the wishes of her husband. She resented Bemidji. It was boring and she had nothing to look forward to. Coming from a wealthy family, she was used to the high life and the constant excitement of being in New York – the city that never sleeps.

For many years, she resented Ryan's decision. Ryan had no choice. He wasn't able to make enough money if he works in New York. Nadia proposed that they take some money from her father but Ryan was too proud. He was brought up in a traditional Christian family where a man should never use the help of his in-laws.

For more than a decade, the both of them suffered. Nadia was resentful and Ryan had to deal with it. When the marriage hit the twenty year mark, they finally had it. Nadia decided to file for divorce. She was someone who loves the children and had stayed for a long time. In fact, she had wanted a divorce for more than ten years.

That's when Ryan started to realize his nightmare. Being resentful, Nadia went to get one of the best lawyers in the country. Her father funded her legal needs. She wanted to make sure that Ryan pays for it. She was successful and managed to get a sizeable amount of alimony. He was required to pay 60% of his take home pay to her.

The worst has yet to come. Because of the length of marriage, the court ordered a lifetime alimony payment. This means that 60% of his take home pay would be deducted each month.

It was a miserable decision that would impact his life over the next few years. What's worse was that he would have minimal rights over seeing his children. The court only allowed him to see his children once a month.

At the age of fifty, it was too much for Ryan to endure.

Chapter 2: The Horrible Impact Of Alimony

I hope I don't paint a negative picture to you, but such situations can be pretty common. Of course, it doesn't even need to be a wealthy woman you married to. There are plenty of cases where the ex-wife takes advantage of the situation to claim a very sizeable alimony payment.

For Ryan, things got tough from then on. He was forced to sell his house in Bemidji and even that, he had to give part of the proceeds

www.singledaddydating.com

to his ex-wife. His ex-wife moved into another house with the children – a seven-bedroom mansion in New York. Meanwhile, Ryan was struggling to make ends meet.

Every income he had needed to be 'taxed' 60% to Nadia. He needed to pay for housing rental, food and other expenses. Worst still, he seemed to lose all passion for life.

He seemed to lose his children and struggled to cope with the situation. It was even tougher because he was someone who wasn't used to expressing his emotions. His siblings didn't know how to help him at all.

Truth is, the impact of alimony goes beyond the numbers. It is something which would also impact the psyche of a man. It makes him feel vulnerable and depressed. It challenges his viewpoint of the world. This is why I understand when there are certain single fathers who are resentful when thinking of alimony.

Simply put, alimony can be unjust because of the terrible impacts it would have to a man.

There are many men suffering in silence from the impact of their divorce. Women are different from men when dealing with a divorce. Women would have their friends and relatives who are ready to support her with everything she needs. She can complain all she wants about the ex-husband and everyone would support her.

Being a man after a divorce is different. Men are not that expressive. We are brought up in a society where we try to be as reserved as possible with our emotions. Because of that, we suffer in silence. Alimony is something that heaps on the pain of divorce.

This book isn't to frighten you about a divorce. There are times where a divorce is what it takes for you to be happy again. However, this is a guide for you to better understand how alimony works and what you can do to better prepare for the situation. I can't be writing about ways for you to pay lesser alimony, because I'm not qualified to do that.

What I'm qualified however, is my experience. I have spoken to many men who have dealt with their divorce and have problems with these situations, many of them would be situations you would have to deal with in the future.

One great guide that many single fathers I know have used is Men's Divorce Tactics. Personally, I haven't checked up this course yet, but there are other single fathers are in awe with this course for how it has helped them in the past.

Check it out at:

www.singledaddydating.com/divorcetactics/

Chapter 3: Understand The Different Types Of Alimony

Every state have their own laws for deciding whether alimony would be paid. Having said that, you should know that the judge can also use judicial discretion when dealing with such issues. When deciding alimony, these factors are normally considered:-

- Duration of the marriage

- Potential earning capacity of both

spouses

- Ability of one spouse to pay

- Age, mental, emotional and physical of each spouse

- Whether or not the custodial parent would earn less because of the duty to take care of the child/children

If the marriage has been for a long time and both you and your ex-wife works, while having comparable income and pension plans; then there might be no alimony. However, the dynamics changes if you both have been married for a long time and your ex-wife is a stay-at-home mum who doesn't have any skills for work.

For most states, a 'long-term marriage' is defined by a marriage of more than 10 years. The types of alimony that you would need to pay would depend on the financial situation in the marriage. Here are the various types of alimony:-

- **Permanent Alimony.** Permanent alimony would be paid to the recipient until the death of the one paying or if the recipient remarries. Even if the recipient remarries, there are some situations where alimony would still need to pay. Such alimony happens when the marriage is for a long term and the recipient has a disability that keeps her from working again. For such alimony payments, there could be an adjustment upwards or downwards, depending on the situation. This could be an increase in salary or a change of jobs which pays a higher salary; this would be an increase in alimony. If there is a sudden loss of job, then a decrease in alimony might be applied for.

- **Temporary Alimony.** Temporary alimony would only last a set period of time. This is normally when a divorce causes a temporary financial challenge for a spouse. This alimony would be awarded until that spouse can recover financially. The length of time for alimony payments would be determined by state laws.

- **Rehabilitative Alimony.** Rehabilitative Alimony is awarded when the spouse needs some assistance with job training or college expenses. The purpose is so that she could eventually return to the job force after the divorce. Many wives who have been a stay at home mother would need some time to develop skills after many years of not working. This enables the spouse to take classes and special job training so they won't need to be dependent on alimony. Like temporary alimony, these kind of alimony are also for a set period of time.

- **Reimbursement Alimony.** Such alimony is paid in certain situations where a spouse have helped the other in certain expenses. This may include a spouse helping the other pay for his college tuition. These payments had been crucial in building the other spouse's career. The payments can be made over a period of time or in a lump sum.

When it comes to understanding the different types of alimony, you would need a lawyer to explain to you the specific law in your state. However, all states in the United States follow these similar standard in alimony. There might be slight changes here and there, but they are essentially the same.

You would still need to check with your lawyer for proper guidance.

Chapter 4: 7 Commonly Asked Questions On Alimony

Many single fathers come to ask me questions about alimony and it often amazes me. I would wonder "What value can I even give you?"

It wasn't until the past few years that I realize how valuable my advice can be. I'm not a lawyer who is qualified to talk to you about it. However, what I have is the empathy and experience to share with you my understanding.

Most of the questions are more or less the same. They are normally asked by single fathers who have no idea what to expect. These 7 questions are the most common questions you would have as a man going through a divorce. I have been asked about this various times and I'm sure it would have come across your mind.

Question 1: Why does my state use spousal support instead of alimony?

They are all the same actually. Many men actually get confused but they are the same thing. It can also mean 'spousal maintenance'. Don't worry, you won't have to make two payments!

Question 2: What are the different types of alimony?

I have already covered this in the previous chapter, but the two most common are temporary and permanent alimony. The main factor that determines whether it is temporary or permanent is the length of marriage.

Question 3: How long would I need to pay alimony?

Again, I have already answered this. Permanent alimony would be for your entire life (a real nightmare!) while temporary would be determined on various factors, based on your state's legislation.

Question 4: What happens when my ex-wife remarries?

Generally, alimony would stop once an ex-

ries (YAHOO!). However, there are certain situations where alimony would still need to be paid. This is rare though.

Question 5: Are only men responsible for alimony?

This is perhaps the ultimate question when asking about alimony.

No. Men aren't the only one responsible for alimony. There are cases where women pay alimony too.

However, most alimony payments are made to the women. In fact, it wouldn't be too much to say that 99% of alimony payments are made from the man to the woman.

The only instant where women pay for alimony is when the man is a stay-at-home father and the women is the breadwinner in the family. Not too common in a typical

Western family.

Question 6: How much alimony would I need to pay?

This depends on the court and the various factors that come into play. Your income and obligations would normally be the main factors being considered.

Question 7: What happens when I lose my job?

You would be entitled to alimony modification. These is tricky though. Even if the court may most likely grant a modification, it would change your life too. Now, you have zero income. How would you expect to pay your ex-wife a percentage of zero?

The court won't simply allow you to NOT

pay alimony.

You would also need to prove to the court that you are actively looking for a job.

Chapter 5: How Are Alimony Payments Determined

When it comes to determining alimony, many factors come into play. The first thing to consider when determining the obligation you have to your ex-wife would be your ability to pay alimony. Yours and your ex-wife's gross income would be looked at, and then mandatory deductions being subtracted.

This would be the net income.

Among the mandatory deductions include items such as social security, health care and income taxes. Other items such as union dues or social dues which are work-related wouldn't be deducted as they aren't mandatory.

When it comes to alimony, the courts place a higher priority on alimony payments than voluntary debt. What this means is that you have to pay your alimony payments before paying your voluntary debts.

Other factors that come into play in determining alimony include:-

- **Ability To Earn.** Both spouses ability to earn would also need to be taken into account. The amount of money a spouse actually earns isn't only considered, but his/her potential for making money is carefully considered too.

- **Standard Of Living While Married.**

Ideally, the standard of living should be maintained even after the divorce. The court would make it an aim that there won't be changes in this as much as possible. That becomes the ultimate aim of alimony – to make sure that your ex-wife's standard of living remained the same.

- **Length Of Marriage.** These is perhaps the main factor in determining if the alimony is a temporary or permanent. If the marriage is relatively short and if there aren't any children, the court may refuse to grant alimony. Should there be children who is younger (below the age of five), the courts would normally award alimony to the spouse given physical custody. This is because the courts normally recommend having a full-time parent at home.

- **Debts.** During the divorce, the court would allocate the debts incurred during the marriage between the two spouses. It would be proportioned based on who benefits the most from the asset that came with the debt. Should the court orders a spouse to pay a large portion of the debt, it would reduce the amount of alimony required to be paid.

- **Tax Consequences.** For federal income tax purposes, alimony which is approved by the court is deductible (for you) and taxable to your ex-wife.

Another important factor that would come into consideration is whether or not the spouse receiving the alimony would have the ability to make money. Their ability to support themselves is important when determining the amount of alimony being paid.

Whether or not a spouse has marketable skills and being able to work is something important. The location where the custodial parent stays is also important. If she stays at a place without proper child care and the child is still young, she would need to receive more alimony because she doesn't have the time to work.

There is a difference between being able to self-support and self-supporting.

If a spouse has marketable skills, have the time to work but refuses to work; the court would limit the alimony. This impacts the alimony amount and the length of it too.

If your ex-wife becomes self-supporting before the end of the court ordered support period, you can petition to the courts to terminate the alimony. The other way is allowed too. Your ex-wife can apply for an extension of the alimony, if she has trouble supporting herself.

Chapter 6: How Alimony Can Be Modified

There is a possibility of alimony modification should there be a substantial change in needs or changes in the ability to pay. Even if the alimony has been judged to be of a certain amount, this figure can still change if it can be proved on certain basis.

If it can be proven that the needs of the ex-wife has increased, then the alimony would be increased. The same goes if there is an increase in the ability to pay of the paying spouse.

When dealing with modification, there is a possibility of increasing, decreasing or terminating the alimony payments altogether. These are common reasons why there is an alimony modification:-

• Cost Of Living Adjustment Clauses

There could be included in the original divorce agreement that states that alimony would increase at a rate equal to the cost of living. Should there be such a clause in the original agreement, there wouldn't be a constant need to modify the alimony.

• Agreement To Modify Alimony

You can come to an agreement with your ex-wife to modify the terms of the alimony. Although this can be done without the court's approval, it could create problems if the ex-wife refuses to honor the agreement. Ideally, you should make sure that the agreement is signed by a judge to enforce it.

• Escalator Clause

An escalator clause could be included in the original divorce agreement. This is to ensure that the alimony recipient receives an automatic share of any increase in the payer's earning. If you as a payer receives an annual increase in your salary, your ex-wife would have a similar increase in alimony receipts as well.

• Temporary Modification

There are certain situations that would cause temporary difficulties in a person's life. Such situations such as a loss of job, terminal diseases or other unexpected conditions would create such situations. If the alimony recipient has suddenly become ill, then the court would increase the amount of support for a temporary period. After the period ends, the alimony payment changes back to the previous amount.

***

If the alimony recipient has a substantial increase in income, the payer can request a downward modification of alimony based on the change in circumstance.

There are other changes that would impact the amount of alimony being paid. These circumstances arise from other factors, such as:-

- **New Support Responsibilities.** If you (as an alimony payer) remarries and have another child, the court may reduce alimony payment to your ex-wife. However, this doesn't apply if you take on a stepchild.

- **Changes In Law.** There are times where changes in law impact the amount of alimony paid. However, this isn't too common.

- **Financial Difficulties.** Should there be a sudden financial emergency, such as needing to pay a huge medical bill or some other unexpected emergency, the alimony can be requested for a decrease. An increase can also happen if the alimony recipient have the same difficulties.

- **Increase In Cost Of Living.** When inflation reduces the value of the alimony paid, the recipient may request for an alimony modification based on the increase. The court would determine the appropriate increase in alimony.

- **Disability.** If the recipient or payer finds it difficult to support him/herself due to a physical or mental condition, the alimony may be modified as well. If the payer has a disability, the alimony can be requested for a decrease. If the recipient has disabilities, the alimony can be requested for an increase.

- **Decreased Need For Support.** When the recipient need for support decreases, the court would reduce or terminate alimony payments if the payer requests for it. This happens when the recipient gets a higher paying job or gets married.

All these factors can easily impact the alimony payment. However, it is still up to the court's discretion to reduce the amount of alimony paid. You would need to speak to your lawyer on whether you can reduce alimony based on your situation.

In the past few years, there have been many lawyers who have frequent our single father support groups. They have advised us on the various situations.

One major advice lawyers always give is to always stay updated with the law. There would be some changes that can reduce the alimony you pay. Alimony can be easily modified with the right arguments in court.

Chapter 7: Tax Impact Of Alimony

When it comes to the tax impact of alimony, the treatment is as follows:-

- It is a taxable income for the recipient. Report on Form 1040 Line 11.

- It is a deductible expense for the payer. Report on Form 1040 Line 31.

This is the general tax treatment for alimony in the United States.

As a single father, although you would tend to be paying alimony, it is important to understand the tax treatment for the recipient (your ex-wife) as well.

For the recipient, the full amount of alimony received during the year would be reported. The recipient don't have to report the child support amount received because it is a non-taxable income. Reporting alimony is mandatory and failure to report would result in an IRS audit.

As the person paying the alimony, this represents a tax deduction. You need to report the total amount of alimony you paid during the year. Don't include child support payments because it isn't tax-deductible and not reported in your federal tax return.

For a single father, alimony would represents quite a huge figure. However, for it to become tax deductible, the following six requirements would need to be met first:-

1. You and your wife (or ex-wife) don't

file a joint tax return.

2. Your payment is in cash.

3. The divorce instrument doesn't say that the payment is NOT alimony.

4. If legally separated, you and your ex-wife shouldn't be members of the same household when making payment.

5. You have no liability to make any cash or property payments after the death of your wife or ex-wife.

6. This payment isn't treated as child support.

As this alimony payments can be quite huge, you would need to keep a record of this to claim for tax. I have seen single fathers paying more than half of their salary to their ex-wives. Imagine how big a tax deduction that would be.

For someone who is filing for tax, there are

certain considerations to take into account when it is tax period. Among the things to consider include:-

- **Filing Status.** Your marital status towards the end of the year determines your filing status. Once you have a divorce agreement and final decree, then only can you file as single.

- **Head Of Household.** You can file as the head of household after the divorce, because this would decrease your tax obligation. To qualify, you need to fulfil these conditions:-

  i. You have paid at least half of the cost of keeping up the home during the year.

  ii. The home has been the main home for you and your children for at least half the year.

  iii. Your spouse hasn't lived in the home

for at least half the year.

- **Divorce Fees.** Legal fees aren't deductible in your tax returns. They are considered as a personal expense.

- **Child Tax Credit And Dependent Care Credit.** The parent who can claim child tax credit is the parent who claims exception for the child. If you are the non-custodial parent, you can't claim the dependent care credit even if you are eligible to claim the child's exemption. In short, dependent care credit is meant for the custodial parent while child tax credit is dependent upon who claims for it.

It is crucial for you to meet with a tax expert to discuss about your situation. Be honest with them and see how they can help you. Remember to also check your local tax authorities to see if you can save on your tax payable.

As a single father, your finances might already be very tight. You need to maintain your discipline with your finances. Due to your high alimony payments, knowing the proper tax treatment for your alimony can save you quite a bit of money in terms of tax payable.

Chapter 8: Alimony Jokes

Alimony is tough on single fathers. However, it doesn't mean that you can't take a light-hearted view on it.

Often, when you start to take a lighter-heart viewpoint on a subject, it becomes easier to manage. In this chapter, I would share some popular alimony jokes that some of my fellow friends share.

***

My ex-wife was a heart surgeon. She ripped my heart out.

My husband and I divorced because of religious difference. She believed she was God. I didn't.

Marriage is a three-ring circus – engagement RING, wedding RING and suffer-RING.

Make love, not war. Hell! Do both, get married!

Marriage is the only war where you sleep with the enemy.

She was a great housekeeper, too. When we divorced, she kept the house.

Why is divorce so expensive? Because it is worth it.

Marriage is great, but I wouldn't recommend it to single people.

What is alimony?

The screwing you get for the screwing you got!

A man and his wife were in divorce court, trying to win custody of the children. The mother tells the judge that since she brought the children to the world, she should have full custody of them.

The man also wanted custody over the children, so the judge asked him for justification. After a long silence, the man rose from his chair and replied:

"Your honor, when I put a dollar into the vending machine and a soda comes out, does the soda belongs to the machine or me?"

Husband 1: My wife is an angel

Husband 2: You're lucky. Mine's still alive!

My wife and I were happy for twenty-five years… then we met each other.

Marriage – Five minutes to get in, a lifetime to get out.

Chapter 9: How Pete Managed To Save On Alimony

This is a personal story from Pete. He is a sweet-tempered Canadian who has been divorced five years back.

The court ordered him to pay half of his monthly take home pay. However, he managed to convince the ex-wife to accept only 15% of his monthly take-home pay. This is his story.

"I wasn't happy with paying alimony. 50% of my monthly salary! How is that fair? I need to pay for the mortgage on the house she is staying in and the court decides to take away half of my monthly pay. Together with the mortgage, I would be left with less than 20%!

What the hell!

That was when I took my anger to work. It took me slightly under a year to make my 'plan' work. But it worked, and that's the most important.

My ex-wife and I separated very tensely. We have been contemplating divorce for more than a year when she decided to file. I was angered when she filed. I always thought that it was simply a threat but when it happened, I knew I needed to do something.

Things got worse when the court judged that I should pay half of my monthly salary to her. I didn't like it at all. In fact, who the hell likes paying half of their monthly salary to another person they don't like?

I took time to read up as many stories of alimony as possible. I read case laws to determine what would make the court change its mind about alimony. I was determined not to let my ex-wife's greed take over my life.

I found out that I may not need to pay alimony if I can convince the court that she is capable of working. I knew she could work. She could probably make more than what she is receiving from alimony. I knew she was simply lazy. Her excuse that she 'needed to take care of the son' was a weak excuse.

She haven't been working for five years, ever since my son was born. She was a nurse in the past and I knew that it was a good job to have. I got documents regarding her previous salary and a projected salary if she works again. I realized that she could be making way more money than what she received in alimony.

That was the first step: Convincing the court that she can work.

I knew her excuse would be that she needed to take care of the son. I did my homework. I checked around the cost of childcare. I had a plan to convince the court *about her viability of her working.*

Next, I set up a 529 plan for my son. I wanted the court to know that I am a responsible father who has a plan for my son. I would convince the court that I simply can't afford to pay so much in alimony when I am contributing to the 529 plan.

Next, I set about to find a smaller house for her to stay in. She is staying in a house which has four bedrooms and three bathrooms. Why does she need such a big house? Even worse was the fact that I was paying the mortgage on that house and only the both of them stay in there.

I look for houses which are smaller. I would convince the court that I want to save more money for my child's future.

The last step would be to convince her to date again. I managed to convince her sister to set her up on dates. Not long, she was in a serious relationship with another man. The both of them were dating for three months when I executed the 'final move' of my plan.

I went to court to seek modification of alimony. I have been working on this plan for almost a year. I convinced the court that my ex-wife was simply being lazy, that she didn't need such a big house and that I was putting my child's best interest at heart. What makes things bad for her was that she was dating the other guy. It reflected that she didn't suffer much from the divorce.

From there, I managed to cut down my alimony payments from 50% to 15%. It took me some time, but I managed to do it.

Ever since, my ex-wife was back at work. I have joint custody with her. She is looking to get married soon, but most importantly, I pay less alimony. I might consider applying to the court to forgo alimony once she gets married. That's the plan."

***

Pete's story illustrates how you can save on alimony. It doesn't mean that you should be mean to your ex-wife. What this means is that you get to limit the damages done from the past. Perhaps the reason why you had to pay such a high alimony in the first place was because the both of you were highly emotional from the divorce. She wanted you to pay.

There are times when the ex-wife is simply greedy and lazy. You can't fall for such behavior. That was what Pete did. His plan worked and I am happy for him. Alimony don't have to be detrimental to your financial life. You can still do something with it, if you have a better understanding of it. As a single father, I wish you the best of luck.

LEAVE A REVIEW

I hope this book has helped you well. It isn't my intention at all to go deep into the topic. I am no expert in everything. However, I have the help of many other single fathers who have shared with me their invaluable experience.

If this book has helped you in any way, do leave me a review. This helps build our single father community.

If you feel that this book can be improved in any way, do mention it in the review. I would love to hear from you.

I wish you luck as a single father…

ABOUT NICK THOMAS

Nicholas Thomas has helped many single fathers cope with divorce in the past few years. By helping them gain more confidence and stability in their lives, he is able to guide them towards being a man that attracts other women easily.

He divorced back in 2008 and knows how difficult a divorce can be for a man. It was a terrible time for him when he got his divorce. He envisioned his children blaming him and not being able to spend time with him. It gave him a constant guilt trip.

Being a divorced man can be very difficult. Ever since his 'emotional recovery' from the divorce, he has helped many single fathers by advising and helping them gain confidence.

Should you want to share your story with him, you can do so at
www.singledaddydating.com/shareastory/

ALSO BY NICK THOMAS

(1) Dating After Divorce For The Single Daddy

(2) Dating Ideas For The Single Daddy

(3) How To Be An Alpha Male

(4) First Date Conversations

(5) Online Dating

(6) How To Approach Women

(7) Mature Dating

(8) Single Parent Support

(9) Coping With Divorce

(10) Parenting After Divorce

Visit www.singledaddydating.com/bookstore/

Get Your Complimentary
FREE BOOK

Join our community today and get **10 Crucial
Checklist To Dating Success For Single Fathers**
FREE, delivered right to your email…

JOIN US AT
WWW.SINGLEDADDYDATING.COM/
NEWSLETTER/